The Pileated Woodpecker

The Pileated Woodpecker

By Seliesa Pembleton

DILLON PRESS, INC.
Minneapolis, Minnesota 55415

Photographic Acknowledgments

The photographs are reproduced through the courtesy of: T.J. Cawley/Tom Stack & Associates (p. 21); Isidor Jeklin (pp. 18, 47, 49); G. LeBaron/Vireo (p. 34); Lee Kuhn (pp. 36, 41); Mike McHugh/Cornell Laboratory of Ornithology (p. 32); Leonared Lee Rue III (p. 11); F.K. Schleicher/Vireo (p. 23); and Ted Willcox (pp. 8, 13, 15, 26, 30, 52, 54). Cover photo by Isidor Jeklin. Title page photo by Ted Willcox.

Library of Congress Cataloging-in-Publication Data

Pembleton, Seliesa.
    The pileated woodpecker / by Seliesa Pembleton.
    (A Dillon remarkable animals book)
    Includes index.
    Summary: Introduces the appearance, habitat, and behavior of the pileated woodpecker, discusses the impact humans have had on the bird and its habitat, and describes a year in the life of the woodpecker.
    ISBN 0-87518-392-1

    1. Pileated woodpecker—Juvenile literature. [1. Pileated woodpecker. 2. Woodpeckers.] I. Title. II. Series.
    QL696.P56P46   1989
    598'.72—dc 19   88-20220
                                                                 CIP
                                                                  AC

Dillon Press, Inc., 242 Portland Avenue South
Minneapolis, Minnesota 55415

Printed in the United States of America
    2 3 4 5 6 7 8 9 10 98 97 96 95 94 93 92 91 90 89

Contents

Facts about the Pileated Woodpecker

Scientific Name: *Dryocopus pileatus*

Description:

Length—16 to 19.5 inches (41 to 50 centimeters)

Wing Span—27 to 30 inches (69 to 77 centimeters)

Weight—10 to 16 ounces (283 to 454 grams)

Physical Features—Feet have two toes pointed forward, and two pointed backward; bill is heavy and chisel-like; tongue is retractable and barb-tipped; two central tail feathers are stiff to support the bird's body against tree trunks

Color—Black body, red crest, white throat and neck stripes, black bill, white patches on underwing

Distinctive Habits: Communicates with loud, cackling call and rhythmic pounding on hollow trees; chisels nest and roost cavities in trees

Food: Wild berries, fruits, nuts, and insects, especially carpenter ants and the wormlike larvae of wood-boring beetles

Reproductive Cycle: Pairs mate for life; in April, female lays eggs which hatch in about 18 days; male and female share duties of hatching and raising young

Life Span: One bird marked with a metal band was found to have lived 12 years

Range: Woodlands of the eastern half of the United States from Florida to Canada, of Canada, and of the northwestern United States

The shaded area on this map shows the range of the pileated woodpecker.

Chapter 1

Life on the Side of a Tree

Imagine what your life would be like if you spent much of the day hanging from the side of a tree, pounding your lips into the hard, rough bark. What would keep you from falling off the tree? Would you always have a terrible headache? How would you eat? If you were a woodpecker, you wouldn't have to worry about any of these problems.

Toes and Tail

Pileated (*PY-lee-ayt-ehd* or *PIHL-ee-ayt-ehd*) woodpeckers are suited to life on the side of a tree trunk. These birds have short, strong legs and four strong toes on each foot. Their feet are **zygodactylous***, which means that they have two toes pointed

---

*Words in **bold type** are explained in the glossary at the end of this book.

forward and two toes pointed backward. Each toe ends in a long, sharp, curved claw that tightly grips the bark on a tree.

Even with strong toes and strong leg muscles, a woodpecker needs another aid to help it cling to trees. Two stiff, spiny-tipped feathers in the center of the bird's tail press against the tree trunk as the bird rests or climbs. These tail feathers also give the woodpecker a stable brace for heavy hammering.

A Sharp Beak and Hard Head

Whap, whap, whap! Chips fly as the big, red-crested woodpecker hammers into the side of a tree. Any bird that chisels away tree bark and wood needs a large, hard, pointed beak. A long, strong neck thrusts the bird's head back and forth rapidly as it rips into the tree. A thick skull and muscles pad the bird's brain, eyes, and ears so they are not injured by the heavy pounding. Short, thick, bristle feathers cover the woodpecker's **nostrils** to keep splin-

10 Zygodactylous, or four-toed, feet and stiff tail feathers help pileated woodpeckers cling to trees.

ters from flying up the bird's nose as it hammers.

The bird may use its heavy bill to chisel out a **cavity**, or hole, in the side of a tree. Woodpeckers sleep, take shelter during bad weather, and raise their young in tree cavities that are high above the ground. A cavity must be big to fit the large pileated woodpecker, and making each hole requires a great deal of heavy pounding.

The pileated woodpecker must also do a lot of hammering in order to satisfy its hearty appetite. The bird hunts for tasty insects, such as carpenter ants and beetle grubs, under the bark of trees. It also eats nuts, wild berries, and other fruits that it may find in its territory. One scientist found a male pileated woodpecker with 469 carpenter ants in its stomach. A female had eaten 153 ants, a beetle, and 17 wild grapes.

An Amazing Tongue

As it searches for food, the pileated woodpecker flies from tree to tree in the forest. Landing near

12   With their powerful neck muscles and hard beaks, pileated woodpeckers can quickly chisel away wood.

the base of a tree, the woodpecker then hops up the trunk in a jerky motion. The bird cocks its bright head and listens for the sound of insects crawling through or gnawing on the wood inside. When it hears such a sound, the woodpecker begins to pound loudly, chiseling a hole into the tree. Finally, the hole is drilled, and out comes the bird's long, slender, probing tongue.

The woodpecker's tongue stretches far beyond the end of the beak as it reaches inside the hole. It has a hard, spearlike point with tiny barbs on the tip. If the woodpecker stabs a juicy beetle grub, the backward-pointing barbs will hook into the grub's soft, white body as the tongue drags out the wiggling snack. A large black carpenter ant may simply stick to the surface of the bird's tongue, which is wet with gluey **saliva**.

Where does the woodpecker keep such a long tongue? This amazing creature coils its tongue around its skull! At the back of the bird's mouth, the tongue is attached to special **hyoid bones**.

The pileated woodpecker's long, sticky, barb-tipped tongue can reach insects hidden deep within trees.

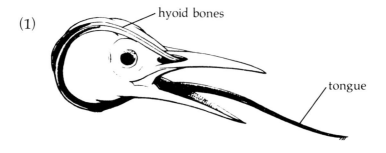

(1) hyoid bones

tongue

(2)

nostril

(3)

At the back of the pileated woodpecker's mouth, the tongue divides into two branches which wrap around the back of the skull. They are joined to the flexible hyoid bones which are anchored in the right nostril. The system of muscles and bones slides forward to extend the tongue (figures 1 and 2), then slides back to pull the tongue into the mouth (figure 3).

These long, thin, flexible bones wrap around the back of the skull and across the top of the bird's head. Here they join together and are anchored in the right nostril. Muscles attached to the hyoids stretch to extend the tongue, and then contract to pull the tongue back into the mouth.

Their specialized toes, tails, beaks, and tongues set woodpeckers apart from other birds. And, in many ways, the pileated woodpecker stands out as an unusual member of its family.

Chapter 2

Knock, Knock.
Who's There?

Is it the Indian hen, the laughing woodpecker, or the carpenter bird? These are all names early explorers and settlers gave to the pileated woodpecker. Today, people still use these common names, as well as others, such as great black woodpecker, cock-of-the-woods, woodcock, and woodchuck.

Common names such as these can be confusing, because one creature may be known by many names, or animals that are quite different may be known by the same name. For example, a bushy-tailed ground squirrel is also called a woodchuck, and a woodcock is best known as a long-billed, brown-striped bird. Sometimes it is difficult to know exactly what animal a person is describing.

Dryocopus pileatus has been known by many different names.

The Red-capped Tree Chopper

Scientists have a more organized method of studying **organisms**, or living things. They give every organism a two-part Latin name, which may be determined by special features of the organism. No matter what language they speak, scientists from all over the world use the same scientific name when they refer to a certain living thing.

The scientific name for the pileated woodpecker is *Dryocopus pileatus (dry-AHK-oh-puhs py-lee-AYT-uhs)*. The word *drys* means "tree" and *kopis* means "cleaver" or "chopper." *Pileum* is the Latin word for a cap with no brim. Put these names together, and this bird is called a red-capped tree chopper.

In addition to the bright red crest on its head, *Dryocopus pileatus* has other special features that make it different from all other North American woodpeckers. A white throat and a white stripe on the neck appear very bright on its black body. On the underside of its wings are large white patches

20

A red forehead and mustache set the male pileated woodpecker apart from the female, whose forehead and mustache are black.

that can be seen clearly when the bird flies.

How can you tell the male pileated woodpecker from the female? He is the one with the red mustache! **Ornithologists**, scientists who study birds, call the stripe of color next to a bird's beak a mustache. The female has a mustache, too, but hers is black. She also has a black forehead, while the male's forehead is red. In all other ways, the birds of both sexes look alike.

A Big Bird

A pileated woodpecker is probably the largest woodpecker in North America. From the tip of its black beak to the end of its tail, the bird measures 16 to 19.5 inches (41 to 50 centimeters) long. The span from wing tip to wing tip is 27 to 30 inches (69 to 77 centimeters).

As with most birds, the pileated woodpecker has bones that are hollow, like pieces of dried macaroni, to keep its body light for flight. Even with its hollow bones, this big bird weighs 10 to 16 ounces (283 to 454 grams).

Because they are such large birds, pileated woodpeckers have to be strong fliers. Their wings stroke like oars through the air: *flap, flap, flap.* They may also use a flight pattern like that of other woodpeckers. They stroke a few times, fold their wings next to their bodies, and glide "downhill"

Large white patches on the underside of the wings and two stiff tail
feathers are visible as the pileated woodpecker flies.

through the air: *flap, flap, flap—glide; flap, flap, flap—glide.*

As the bird travels above the treetops, looking somewhat as if it is riding an invisible roller coaster, it may shriek a loud cackle. A bird-watcher soon learns to identify this bird call because it is unlike any other.

The red-crested creature may also send messages through the forest by beating on a "drum"—a hollow tree trunk or branch. While other woodpeckers make a light tapping sound, the pileated woodpecker hammers a deep drumming that echoes quite a distance through the woods.

In North America, many of the common woodpecker relatives are also black, red, and white. The red-headed woodpecker is the only woodpecker in the United States with an entirely red head and neck. The red-bellied woodpecker has a smooth, red cap on its head and a few reddish feathers on its belly. Hairy woodpeckers are black and white, and the males have a small, red patch on the back of the head, while females have no red markings. The tiny downy woodpecker is a carbon copy of the hairy woodpecker, but it is smaller.

The ivory-billed woodpecker, like the pileated woodpecker, has a red crest and black body, but is slightly larger. A white or ivory bill and white patches on the top of its wings also set it apart from its cousin. In the United States, the ivory-billed woodpecker is very rare, and may be **extinct**—no longer living.

With its loud cackling and drumming, its large size, and its bright coloring, the pileated woodpecker stands out among all other woodpeckers. This colorful creature made its home in the vast forests of North America long before the first explorers came to the New World.

Chapter 3

Home Is Where the Trees Are

Centuries ago, when the first European explorers and settlers arrived in the New World, the land beyond the beaches and marshes was covered with forests. Giant, ancient oaks stretched their limbs high into the sky. Their far-reaching branches and leaves cast dark shadows on the sprouts, saplings, young growing trees, old dead trees, and rotting stumps below.

This is exactly what pileated woodpeckers need—a forest with large, old trees. It is their **habitat**, the place with the kind of conditions they need to survive. In this forest habitat, a pileated woodpecker establishes a territory for itself and its mate. Here the birds hollow out their separate roost holes, where they sleep and take shelter, and their

A female pileated woodpecker at home in the forest.

nest holes, where they raise their young. Here, also, they find food—crunchy insects such as ants and beetles, as well as juicy grubs, berries, nuts, and acorns. The pair of birds defends their territory by chasing other pileated woodpeckers away.

The total geographic area in which pileated woodpeckers are found, called their **range**, covers large parts of North America. Pileated woodpeckers live in forest habitats throughout the eastern half of the United States, from Florida north to Canada. They are also found in large parts of Canada, and in the northwestern woodlands of the United States.

The Laughing Woodpecker

In 1803, several hundred years after the first European explorers arrived, John James Audubon came from France to live in America. This adventurous young man was fascinated by the wildlife of the great forests.

Young John traded his fancy French silk cloth-

28

ing for buckskin britches. Rifle in hand, he stalked through the woods hunting deer, turkey, and other game for the dinner table. Yet many times he watched without shooting, delighted by the bright and beautiful birds that flitted through the tree-tops. Once he wrote in his journal, "It would be difficult for me to say where I have not met with that hardy inhabitant of the forest, the pileated woodpecker. Even now, when several species of our birds are becoming rare...it is to be found everywhere in the wild woods, although scarce and shy in the peopled districts."

Like Audubon, many early ornithologists noted that *Dryocopus pileatus* was a very common woodpecker. Aside from an occasional hawk, bobcat, or hungry woodsman, the bird had very few enemies.

The pileated woodpecker was sometimes shot and sold as food in city markets. However, Audubon described its flesh as tough and bluish in color, with a strong, disagreeable odor like the ants and

worms on which the bird fed. For obvious reasons, the pileated woodpecker did not become a popular food with people.

This black-bodied woodpecker was also difficult to hunt. As Audubon chased it from the ground, the pileated woodpecker flew "cackling out its laughter-like notes as if delighted to lead you on a wild goose chase in pursuit." When Audubon followed, the bird would alight on the tallest branches and move to the far side of the tree. Then, in silence, it would peek its flaming red head around the tree trunk—"so well does it seem to know the distance at which a shot can reach it." If a hunter did manage to shoot the clever bird, its long claws might cling to the rough bark long after the bird had died. It might be hours before the body finally tumbled to the ground.

The bird's coloring also helped protect it. As a pileated woodpecker hangs from the side of a tree, its black back blends with the dark bark and the leafy shadows. The big bird is further protected by

Early settlers found the clever pileated woodpecker difficult to hunt, and unpleasant to eat.

its size, and its stout beak can deliver a mighty blow to any enemy.

The Forests Disappear

The biggest threat to the pileated woodpecker has been the disappearance of its habitat. The early settlers cut trees for wood to build ships and houses, to heat their homes, and to cook their food. Farmers cut and burned areas of forests to make room for crops. Manufacturers turned trees into lumber and paper. Throughout the land, the woods rang with the sound of axes and saws and the cry of "timber!" Cities began to appear where huge trees had once grown. The drumming and cackling of the pileated woodpecker stopped echoing across much of the forest, especially in New England.

Early **conservationists**—people who work to protect living things and their natural habitats—were worried. Humans cut down the biggest and oldest trees in the forests, leaving mostly small ones standing. These young trees were not large

A pileated woodpecker hammers at a dead tree as it hunts for insects.

33

enough for the woodpecker's roosting and nesting holes, and did not have hollow trunks filled with crawling insects. Pileated woodpeckers, as well as many other wild creatures, were rapidly disappearing.

Today, the story of the pileated woodpecker is not a sad one. Although no one can exactly explain why, the number of pileated woodpeckers is increasing. Their laughing call is heard again throughout more and more of the forests of North America. Maybe these shy forest creatures have learned to adjust to the changes people have made in their forest habitat. Or perhaps the once small saplings have grown large enough to again provide food and shelter for the birds.

Whatever the reason, the pileated woodpecker has **adapted** to its changing habitat. The bird that thrived when John Audubon came to the United States still makes the North American woodlands its home.

Hungry pileated woodpeckers ripped apart this dead tree.

Chapter 4

Time Flies: A Year in the Forest

The first day of January dawns, and the sky brightens from black to gray. A hungry chickadee flits through the gray gloom in a desperate search for something to eat. Surviving the cold night took most of the bird's energy, and it needs to find food soon.

As the sky turns pink, more forest creatures begin their daily search for something to eat. A male pileated woodpecker, which has been sleeping snuggled in his hole atop a dead pine tree, opens his yellow eyes. His bright, red-crested head pops out of the hole, and he looks to the left and to the right.

Kuk-kuk, kuk, kuk-a, kuk, kuk, kuk, kuk! The noisy woodpecker greets the new day as he flashes

A male pileated woodpecker peeks out from his cavity high above the ground.

out of the hole and bounds through the air in his up-and-down flight.

Wucka, wucka, wucka, wucka! answers his mate. She has been sleeping in her own roosting cavity in a nearby tree.

Like the other forest animals, the woodpeckers begin their day searching for food. They must use a great deal of energy to fly and to keep warm in the cold winter air.

Food and Shelter

When the days grew short and the nights became chilly, many of the insects that the forest birds needed for food died. Other insects crawled deep into cracks and crevices of the tree bark or into hollow trees—well out of the reach of most birds. In addition to lacking food, many birds had no shelter from the cold and snow. Because of the scarce food supply and cold weather, many of them flew south for the winter.

But even the cold winter days do not disturb pileated woodpeckers. Their hard beaks and long tongues can reach hidden insects, and their roost cavities help keep them warm and dry. Unlike many other forest birds, pileated woodpeckers do not have to **migrate** south to survive the winter months.

During the cold days of January, the pair of woodpeckers roams their territory, about two miles (three kilometers) along a woodland stream. They hammer at trees, looking for food. When the weather is icy or stormy, they may return to their roost holes for shelter.

Building a Nest Hole

In mid-February, the pair of pileated woodpeckers becomes carpenters. Moving from tree to tree, they tap the wood and listen. The birds are searching for the perfect site to build the nesting cavity where they will raise their babies. Each year, the woodpeckers build a new nest high above the ground in a carefully chosen tree.

It may take as many as thirty days for the pair to hollow out the spot they have selected. They work to chisel out a hole 40 feet (12 meters) above the forest floor in a large sycamore. This tree is dead, but still quite sturdy. With the bark peeled away, the dry, white trunk is just right for drilling. Its location is perfect—close to the stream, and near both of the birds' roosting holes.

Daily, the birds take turns hammering at the white trunk, sending large splinters flying. They chisel the cavity on the south side of the tree, where the sun's warming rays will reach it.

In March, as the weather warms, the woodpeckers hurry to complete their nest hole. When it is finished, the door to the hole is just big enough for a woodpecker to dart through. Inside, the hole is about 8 inches (20.5 centimeters) wide—a little narrower at the top, a little wider at the bottom. The cavity is between 10 and 25 inches (25.6 and 64 centimeters) deep. A few wood chips form a cushion on the bottom.

The male spits out wood chips as he chisels out the nest cavity.

Courting, Breeding, and Hatching

The female eats often to build up energy and extra protein and calcium for her eggs. If the weather remains mild, she will lay her eggs soon.

The male spends more and more time at his drumming spots. He beats large, hollow trunks with his beak, tapping slowly at first, then faster and faster, and then slower again. His mate may answer with her own drumming signal. The male sings a high *kuk, kuk, kuk,* and the female joins in a duet. Other pileated woodpeckers understand these signals and avoid this territory because it is claimed by the pair.

One day the male flies to his mate, and the two hang side by side from the same tree. With jerky hops, they move around the trunk in what appears to be a game of hide-and-seek. With their brilliant red crests standing straight up and their wings spread slightly, their bodies sway in a courtship dance. When they come together to mate, the female's eggs are **fertilized**.

In April, the female lays her first egg in the nest. The thin shell is glossy white. Inside is a cushion of thick, clear liquid surrounding a yellow yolk with a small spot on it. This tiny spot is a **cell** that will grow and divide to become a baby woodpecker. Almost everything the bird needs to develop is contained within the egg's protective shell.

Warmth is its only other need. The mother fluffs her feathers and settles down gently on top of the egg to heat it with her body.

Late in the afternoon, the father flies to the nest. He taps gently at the door. From inside, the mother taps an answer. Then she darts out from the nest hole, and the father takes her place. The male will keep the eggs warm throughout the night. The female searches for one last tasty insect snack, and then flies to her roost hole to sleep.

Inside the Egg—and Out

Each day a new egg appears in the nest, until there are four. For the next eighteen days, the woodpecker parents take turns sitting atop the eggs. Because the male sleeps on the nest each night, he spends the most time "baby-sitting."

As the parents warm the eggs, amazing changes take place inside each smooth, white shell. The single cell divides and becomes a cluster, or group, of cells. The cluster of cells forms a head with eyes, nerves, and blood vessels. A heart begins to beat. Still, this growing creature does not look much like a bird.

As it develops, the tiny woodpecker absorbs the yolk. It is getting crowded inside the shell. The little bird's body is folded and cramped, and it begins to squirm. When the yolk and clear liquid are almost gone, the baby stretches and breathes the bit of air trapped inside one end of its eggshell. Then it begins to peck at the wall of the shell.

The mother, sitting on the eggs, is startled by the movement beneath her. Rising to look under her feathers, she sees four glossy eggs—but one has a small hole in the end!

For hours, the baby pecks at the shell, using a hardened spot on its otherwise soft bill. It pecks and pushes and rests—then begins the struggle again.

Finally, out pokes a bald, pink head with two dark, bulging lumps, one on each side. These bulges are the baby's eyes, and they are sealed shut. Next come two stubby limbs, the baby's wings. The squirming, naked body has bright pink, wrinkled skin covered with small bumps. In a few days, feathers will begin to sprout from these bumps. In the middle of the pink face, a wide, soft beak gapes open. This baby does not look anything like a woodpecker!

Since its long, skinny neck is too weak to hold up the gasping head, the exhausted baby slumps on the bottom of the nest. The mother bird fluffs her feathers and waits for her mate to return. Soon the pink **nestling** is joined by three other newly hatched—and very hungry—pileated woodpeckers.

Raising the Young

In May, the trees are covered with new green growth, and caterpillars chew the fresh leaves. Now finding food for the ever-hungry **hatchlings** is easy. In and out of the nest fly the adult birds, taking turns in a relay race for food.

After gobbling several green caterpillars, the father flies to the nest tree and lands beside the hole. Out flashes the mother, and in darts the father. His strong toes and claws anchor in the wood near the entrance as he hangs head-down and looks at his youngsters. Four blind faces bob on skinny necks as each baby strains to lift its wide-open mouth the highest. They all hungrily chirp and peep for food.

The father sticks his thick, black beak into one of the wide, soft mouths below him. His black body begins to shudder in a pumping motion, his sides heaving in and out. His body has begun to digest the caterpillars he swallowed earlier. Now he pumps this partly digested food into the throat

The ever-hungry nestlings welcome their father with open beaks.

46

of a hungry hatchling. Both parents feed their young this way until after the babies leave the nest.

Like human babies, woodpecker babies eat a lot. But unlike human babies, hatchlings do not wear diapers. The wood chips in the bottom of the nest help soak up moisture. When the babies pass solid waste out of their bodies, it is contained in a thin, flexible sack. A parent bird carries this sack out of the nest with its beak, and drops it while flying away into the woods.

On the eighth day after the babies have hatched, their eyes begin to open. Soon, their pink, wrinkled skin is covered with soft, pale feathers. Now these babies are starting to look more like pileated woodpeckers.

By the twelfth day, the hungry youngsters crowd the opening of the nest hole. They stretch their necks, gazing out at the woodland and eagerly watching for their parents to return with fresh food.

The nestlings take a look at the world outside their nest.

Defending the Family

The female takes time out from her busy schedule of feeding the nestlings to **preen**. She hangs from the side of a tree, resting on her stiff tail feathers. First she rubs her beak in an oily spot on her back. Then she strokes her oiled bill through the feathers to smooth and waterproof them.

A feather falls off as the female preens. Like her mate, she is beginning to **molt**. Through the warm summer months, she will shed her worn-out feathers a few at a time. She will lose only one feather at a time from each wing so she will be balanced for flight. Because the woodpecker depends so much on her tail for support, she will not shed her stiff tail feathers until they are replaced by new ones.

Suddenly, a *kuk! kuk!* startles the female from her preening. Her mate is sounding an alarm! She flings her body into the air and bounds toward the nest cavity.

With head and neck feathers standing straight

out and wings spread to make him look larger, the male sits near the hole and scolds in his loudest voice. What is the danger?

In the leafy shadows, the female spies a long, black snake slowly gliding along a branch toward the nest hole, his forked tongue flicking in the air. He has detected the nest. It looks as if this **predator** intends to make a meal of the woodpecker nestlings.

The female dives to attack the snake with her strong beak: *Whap! Whap!* The snake clings to the branch and coils toward her. The male joins the attack: *Whap! Whap!*

The bruised snake drops to the ground below and slowly slithers away. This snake could never eat a healthy adult bird, but a defenseless youngster would be easy **prey**. Fortunately for the nestlings, their parents were nearby to defend them.

Leaving the Nest

As summer passes, the young woodpeckers leave the nest and learn to fly. Clumsily, they follow

their parents through the trees and beg for food. With a baby clinging close by, a parent may hammer into an ant tunnel and then move aside. That way the hungry youngster can learn to peck at the bark and feed itself.

The family remains together through much of the fall. As the young birds learn how to feed themselves, they depend less and less on their parents.

In November, the youngsters go their separate ways. Miles away in the forest, each young pileated woodpecker hammers out its first roost hole in which it will sleep through the winter nights.

Never again will the youngsters return to the hole where they hatched. But the old nest cavity does not sit empty for long. During the winter, a screech owl or squirrel may move into the abandoned hole. These and other cavity-nesting creatures, such as wood ducks, starlings, or bluebirds, often depend on old woodpecker holes for shelter.

Each young woodpecker seeks a mate. This pair will stay together in their territory for the rest

Young pileated woodpeckers are fed by their parents until they learn how to feed themselves.

of their lives, and will follow the same yearly cycle of life as their parents.

Life in a Changing World

In many ways, pileated woodpeckers are truly re-markable animals. Their bodies are well suited to life on the side of a tree, and their range extends throughout large areas of North America. Over the centuries, these hardy birds have adapted to the changes humans have made in their forest habitat. Today, pileated woodpeckers make their homes in wooded areas of towns and even cities.

These once-shy birds are learning to live with people. If people learn to respect the pileated woodpeckers and their habitat, these red-crested tree choppers will drum their messages, raise their young, and send their calls echoing like laughter through the woodlands for generations to come.

The pale crest of the young pileated woodpecker will be replaced by red feathers when the bird reaches adulthood.

Glossary

adapt—to adjust to changes made in an organism's habitat in order to increase the chances of survival

cavity—a hole chiseled out of a tree which provides shelter for the pileated woodpecker and other forest animals

cell—the smallest unit that forms all living things

conservationist (kahn-sur-VAY-shuh-nihst)—one who studies and works for the preservation and protection of living things and their natural habitats

extinct (ehk-STINGKT)—no longer living anywhere on earth; many animal and plant species have become extinct

fertilize (FURT-uh-lyz)—to combine a sperm and an egg to begin the process that gives life to a new creature

habitat—the area where a plant or animal naturally lives

hatchling—a creature that has recently hatched from an egg

hyoid (HY-oyd) bones—thin, flexible bones attached to the tongue; they wrap around the skull and anchor in the right nostril

migrate—to move with changing seasons from one area or climate to another for feeding or breeding

molt—to shed fur or feathers before they are replaced with new growth

nestling—a young bird that has not yet left the nest

nostrils—openings in the nose that are used for breathing, and, in the case of certain birds, for anchoring the hyoids

organism (OHR-guh-nihz-uhm)—a living thing

ornithologist (ohr-nuh-THAHL-uh-jihst)—a scientist who studies birds

predator (PREHD-uh-tuhr)—an animal that hunts other animals for food

preen—to clean and straighten feathers using the beak

prey—an animal that is hunted by another animal for food

range—the geographic area in which an organism (living thing) may be found

saliva (suh-LY-vuh)—the watery liquid in the mouth which moistens food before swallowing; it can be used to trap small food, such as insects

zygodactylous (zy-goh-DAK-tuh-luhs)—having two toes pointed forward and two toes pointed backward

Index